Wolverineology Trivia Challenge

Michigan Wolverines Football

Wolverineology Trivia Challenge – Michigan Wolverines Football;
Third Edition 2008

Published by
Kick The Ball, Ltd
8595 Columbus Pike, Suite 197
Lewis Center, OH 43035
www.TriviaGameBooks.com

Designed, Formatted, and Edited by: Tom Rippey & Paul Wilson
Researched by: Tom Rippey

*For information on ordering this book in bulk at reduced prices, please email us
at pfwilson@trivianthology.com.*

International Standard Book Number: 978-1-934372-28-9

Printed & Bound in the United States of America

Tom P. Rippey III & Paul F. Wilson

Wolverineology Trivia Challenge

Michigan Wolverines Football

Researched by Tom P. Rippey III

Tom P. Rippey & Paul F. Wilson, Editors

Kick The Ball, Ltd
Lewis Center, Ohio

This book is dedicated to our families and friends for your unwavering love, support, and your understanding of our pursuit of our passions. Thank you for everything you do for us and for making our lives complete.

Dear Friend,

Thank you for purchasing our **Wolverineology Trivia Challenge** game book!

We hope you enjoy it as much as we enjoyed researching and putting it together. This book can be used over and over again in many different ways. One example would be to use it in a head-to-head challenge by alternating questions between Wolverine football fans – or by playing as teams. Another option would be to simply challenge yourself to see how many questions you could answer correctly. No matter how you choose to use this book, you'll have fun and maybe even learn a fact or two about Wolverines football.

We have made every attempt to verify the accuracy of the questions and answers contained in this book. However it is still possible that from time to time an error has been made by us or our researchers. In the event you find a question or answer that is questionable or inaccurate, we ask for your understanding and thank you for bringing it to our attention so that we may improve future editions of this book. Please email us at tprippey@trivianthology.com with those observations and comments.

Have fun playing **Wolverineology Trivia Challenge**!

Tom & Paul

Tom Rippey & Paul Wilson
Co-Founders, Kick The Ball, Ltd

PS – You can discover more about all of our current trivia game books by visiting us online at www.TriviaGameBooks.com.

Table of Contents

How to Play

Book Format:

There are four quarters, each made up of fifty questions. Each quarter's questions have assigned point values. Questions are designed to get progressively more difficult as you proceed through each quarter, as well as through the book itself. Most questions are in a four-option multiple-choice format so that you will at least have a 25% chance of getting a correct answer for some of the more challenging questions.

We've even added an *Overtime* section in the event of a tie, or just in case you want to keep playing a little longer.

Game Options:

One Player -
To play on your own, simply answer each of the questions in all the quarters, and in the overtime section, if you'd like. Use the *Player / Team Score Sheet* to record your answers and the quarter *Answer Keys* to check your answers. Calculate each quarter's points and the total for the game at the bottom of the *Player / Team Score Sheet* to determine your final score.

Two or More Players –
To play with multiple players decide if you will all be competing with each other individually, or if you will form and play as teams. Each player / team will then have its own *Player / Team Score Sheet* to record its answer. You can use the quarter *Answer Keys* to check your answers and to calculate your final scores.

1

The *Player / Team Score Sheets* have been designed so that each team can answer all questions or you can divide the questions up in any combination you would prefer. For example, you may want to alternate questions if two players are playing or answer every third question for three players, etc. In any case, simply record your response to your questions in the corresponding quarter and question number on the *Player / Team Score Sheet.*

A winner will be determined by multiplying the total number of correct answers for each quarter by the point value per quarter, then adding together the final total for all quarters combined. Play the game again and again by alternating the questions that your team is assigned so that you will answer a different set of questions each time you play.

You Create the Game -
There are countless other ways of using **Wolverineology Trivia Challenge** questions. It's limited only to your imagination. Examples might be using them at your tailgate or other college football related party. Players / Teams who answer questions incorrectly may have to perform a required action, or winners may receive special prizes. Let us know what other games you come up with!

Have fun!

1) Has the Michigan football team ever been know by any other nickname besides "Wolverines"?

    A) Yes
    B) No

2) What are the colors for Michigan?

    A) Black and Gold
    B) White and Blue
    C) Maize and Blue
    D) Yellow and Brown

3) What is the name of the stadium where Michigan plays?

    A) Wolverine Field
    B) Schembechler Stadium
    C) Fielding Field
    D) Michigan Stadium

4) How many Heisman trophy winners played at Michigan?

    A) 1
    B) 2
    C) 3
    D) 5

5) What is the name of the Michigan fight song?

    A) "The Victors"
    B) "Rawhide"
    C) "Hail to the Victors"
    D) "Grease Lightning"

6) What trophy does Michigan and Michigan State play for annually?

    A) Johnny Appleseed Trophy
    B) Paul Bunyan Trophy
    C) Governor's Cup
    D) The Michigan Cup

7) Which ex-President of the United States played center for Michigan?

    A) Ronald Regan
    B) Gerald Ford
    C) Dwight Eisenhower
    D) John F. Kennedy

8) Who had the longest coaching tenure at Michigan?

    A) Fielding Yost
    B) Bennie Oosterbaan
    C) Bo Schembechler
    D) Lloyd Carr

9) Michigan has never had two different running backs rush for over 1,000 yards in the same season.

    A) True
    B) False

10) Which Big Ten opponent has Michigan played the most?

    A) Michigan State
    B) Ohio State
    C) Minnesota
    D) Illinois

11) How many times has Michigan appeared in the Rose Bowl?

    A) 13
    B) 15
    C) 17
    D) 20

12) What is the nickname of the stadium where Michigan plays?

    A) The Big House
    B) The Horseshoe
    C) Death Valley
    D) Champions Field

13) What is the name of Michigan's Mascot?

A) Wolvi the Wolverine
B) Huggie Bear
C) Brownie
D) No Mascot

14) What trophy does Michigan and Minnesota play for?

A) Tomahawk Trophy
B) Little Brown Jug
C) Great Lakes Award
D) M State Trophy

15) The stadium seating capacity for Michigan over is 110,000.

A) Yes
B) No

16) What year did Michigan play its first game?

A) 1879
B) 1885
C) 1891
D) 1897

First Quarter   *1-Point Questions*

17) How many bowl bound teams did the Wolverines play in 2007?

- A) 3
- B) 5
- C) 7
- D) 9

18) In the song "The Victors" Michigan is champions of what?

- A) The West
- B) The East
- C) The Midwest
- D) The Big Ten

19) Who holds the career rushing record for Michigan?

- A) Tyrone Wheatley
- B) Anthony Thomas
- C) Jamie Morris
- D) Michael Hart

20) Who was the first consensus All-American at Michigan?

- A) William Cunningham
- B) Tom Harmon
- C) Harry Kipke
- D) Desmond Howard

First Quarter *1-Point Questions*

21) What nickname did the Michigan Marching band earn in 1950 after playing in both Yankee Stadium and the Rose Bowl?

    A) Michigan Pride
    B) America's Band
    C) Transcontinental Marching Band
    D) Band of the Heartland

22) What nickname was Coach Herbert Crisler known by?

    A) Crimson
    B) Fritz
    C) The Man in Blue
    D) H-Back Crisler

23) Who is the coach with the most wins at Michigan?

    A) Gary Moeller
    B) Lloyd Carr
    C) Bo Schembechler
    D) Fielding Yost

24) What year was the first undefeated season for Michigan (minimum 8 games)?

    A) 1898
    B) 1902
    C) 1910
    D) 1925

25) Who holds the record for passing yards in a single game at Michigan?

    A) Jim Harbaugh
    B) John Navarre
    C) Brian Griese
    D) Chad Henne

26) What coach was responsible for the purchase of the Little Brown Jug?

    A) Fielding Yost
    B) Lloyd Carr
    C) Bo Schembechler
    D) Elton Wieman

27) The "wings" on the Michigan helmet were initially painted white.

    A) True
    B) False

28) How many consecutive bowl games has Michigan been to?

    A) 25
    B) 33
    C) 37
    D) 49

29) Have Michigan and Ohio State ever played on a neutral site?

    A) Yes
    B) No

30) Who holds the Michigan record for total yards against Ohio State in a single game?

    A) Tim Biakabutuka
    B) John Navarre
    C) Butch Woolfolk
    D) Tom Brady

31) How many Michigan head coaches have been consensus All-Americans as Michigan football players?

    A) 0
    B) 2
    C) 4
    D) 8

32) Which team has Michigan played the most in bowl games?

    A) Washington
    B) UCLA
    C) Texas
    D) Southern Cal

33) Who has received the most individual national awards while at Michigan?

    A) Tom Harmon
    B) Desmond Howard
    C) Charles Woodson
    D) David Baas

34) What color were Michigan's helmets prior to 1938?

    A) Black
    B) Gray
    C) Red
    D) Blue

35) Who scored the first touchdown for the Wolverines in their 2007 bowl game against Florida?

    A) Michael Hart
    B) Adrian Arrington
    C) Mike Massey
    D) Mario Manningham

36) What is the Michigan team MVP Award called?

    A) The Yost Award
    B) Bo Schembechler Award
    C) Maize and Blue Award
    D) Best Player Award

First Quarter *1-Point Questions*

37) Michigan has a winning percentage of more than 60% against Ohio State.

    A) True
    B) False

38) Against which opponent did the Wolverines score the most points in 2007?

    A) Notre Dame
    B) Florida
    C) Illinois
    D) Purdue

39) Who has the Michigan record for most tackles in a single game against Ohio State?

    A) Bob Mielke
    B) Jarrett Irons
    C) Mike Boren
    D) Tom Stincic

40) What year did the Michigan band first perform on the football field?

    A) 1898
    B) 1905
    C) 1912
    D) 1923

41) How many *AP* National Championships has Michigan been awarded?

    A) 2
    B) 3
    C) 5
    D) 7

42) How many current consecutive winning seasons have the Wolverines had?

    A) 21
    B) 29
    C) 35
    D) 40

43) Who was the opponent in the dedication game for the opening of Michigan Stadium?

    A) Ohio State
    B) Navy
    C) Notre Dame
    D) Eastern Michigan

44) How many Big Ten Championships has Michigan won?

    A) 25
    B) 32
    C) 37
    D) 42

WOLVERINEOLOGY TRIVIA CHALLENGE

45) Who holds the single game rushing record at Michigan?

A) Tyrone Wheatley
B) Ron Johnson
C) Tim Biakabutuka
D) Tony Boles

46) What year did Michigan have the most consensus All-Americans?

A) 1972
B) 1988
C) 1991
D) 2004

47) How many Michigan head coaches lasted just one season?

A) 2
B) 4
C) 7
D) 11

48) Who holds the Michigan record for points scored in a single game?

A) Ron Johnson
B) Tom Harmon
C) Desmond Howard
D) Tyrone Wheatley

49) How many non-QB players for Michigan have won Rose Bowl MVP?

- A) 1
- B) 3
- C) 5
- D) 7

50) What year did Michigan first celebrate a victory over Ohio State?

- A) 1879
- B) 1892
- C) 1897
- D) 1913

First Quarter Wolverine Cool Fact

Francis, Albert, and Alvin Wistert all played for the Wolverines. All three received consensus All-American honors as tackles (Francis 1933, Albert 1942, and Alvin 1948-49). All three wore the same number, number 11 which is now retired in their honor. All three have been inducted into the College Football Hall of Fame. Francis never played football before enrolling at Michigan. Albert had his number retired by the Philadelphia Eagles. A football family if there ever was one!

First Quarter Answer Key

1) B – No (The Michigan football team has always been known as the Wolverines. There are only theories as to why, since wolverines are not found in the wild in the state of Michigan.)

2) C – Maize and Blue (A committee of students selected these colors in 1867.)

3) D – Michigan Stadium (Opened in 1927 at a cost of $950,000.)

4) C – 3 (Tom Harmon won the Heisman in 1940, Desmond Howard in 1991, and Charles Woodson in 1997.)

5) A – "The Victors" (Written in 1898, the song is played when the players enter the field and after every score.)

6) B – Paul Bunyan trophy (This tradition started in 1953 when Gov. Williams announced he would award a 4 foot wooden statue of Paul Bunyan to the winner.)

7) B – Gerald Ford (Ford was voted team MVP in 1934 and also played on the 1932 and 1933 national championship teams.)

8) A – Fielding Yost (25 years, 1901-23, 1925-26)

9) B – False (In 1975 Gordon Bell rushed for 1,390 yards and Rob Little rushed for 1,030 yards.)

10) B – Ohio State (104 games)

11) D – 20 (Second in appearances only to Southern Cal which has 32 appearances.)

12) A – The Big House (Nicknamed due to that fact that Michigan Stadium is the largest non-racing stadium in the United States.)

13) D – No Mascot (Michigan does not have a mascot. However, in 1927 two wolverines were taken to a game in but were too ferocious for a return visit.)

14) B – Little Brown Jug (This is the oldest college football trophy game tradition in the Football Bowl Subdivision.)

15) B – No (Even though announced attendance is regularly over 111,000, the current stadium seating capacity is 107,501.)

16) A – 1879 (A 1-0 victory against Racine.)

17) C – 7 (Oregon, Penn State, Purdue, Illinois, Michigan State, Wisconsin and Ohio State. The Wolverines went 4-3 against these teams.)

18) A – The West ("Hail! Hail! To Michigan, the champions of the West")

19) D – Michael Hart (Hart gained 5,189 yards on 1,015 attempts for a 5.0 average with 41 rushing touchdowns.)

20) A – William Cunningham (center 1898)

21) C – Transcontinental Marching Band

22) B – Fritz (While playing at the University of Chicago, Coach Amos Alonzo Stagg nicknamed him this after a famous violinist Fritz Kreisler.)

23) C – Bo Schembechler (194-48-5 [.796])

24) A – 1898 (10-0)

25) B – John Navarre (389 yards versus Iowa in 2003, 26-49 with 1 interception and 2 touchdowns)

26) A – Fielding Yost (He feared that Minnesota may contaminate Michigan's drinking water during a game in 1903 and sent the manager to buy a 5 gallon jug.)

27) B – False (The wings have always been maize. In 1938 Coach Crisler had the "wings" of the Spalding FH5 leather helmets repainted with maize to help players recognize their teammates on the field.)

28) B – 33 (1974 was the last time Michigan missed a bowl game, after finishing the season 10-1! The next longest streak is Florida State with 26.)

29) B – No

30) D – Tom Brady (1998 346 total yards; 375 yards passing, -29 yards rushing)

31) B – 2 (Harry Kipke 1922, Bennie Oosterbaan 1925-27)

32) D – Southern Cal (8 times in the Rose Bowl [2-6].)

33) C – Charles Woodson (5 total awards; Bednarik, Heisman, Thorpe, Nagurski, and Walter Camp all in 1997.)

34) A – Black

35) D – Mario Manningham (Pulled in a 21 yard touchdown pass from Chad Henne for the first score of the game.)

36) B – Bo Schembechler Award (The name was changed from MVP Award to the Bo Schembechler Award in 1995 with Tim Biakabutuka being the first recipient and Michael Hart winning the award in 2007.)

37) B - False (The Wolverines are 57-41-6 against the Buckeyes for a .577 winning percentage.)

38) D – Purdue (Michigan beat the Boilermakers 48-21.)

39) D – Tom Stincic (23 total tackles in 1968; Michigan 14, Ohio State 50)

40) A – 1898 (The bands first public performance was in 1897 and their first performance on the football field was in 1898.)

41) B – 3 (1947 was awarded after "special" post bowl poll, 1948, and 1997.)

42) C – 40 (Currently the longest streak of consecutive winning seasons in college football. The last losing season was in 1967 when Michigan went 4-6.)

43) A – Ohio State (Michigan defeated the Buckeyes in the dedication game 21-0 in 1927.)

44) D – 42

45) B – Ron Johnson (Ron gained 347 yards on 31 attempts for 11.2 yards per carry vs. Wisconsin in 1968.)

46) D – 2004 (4 consensus All-Americans: Braylon Edwards WR, David Baas OL, Marlin Jackson DB, and Ernest Shazor DB)

47) B – 4 (Murphy Crawford, William Ward, Langdon Lea, and George Little)

48) A – Ron Johnson (Ron recorded 5 rushing touchdowns versus Wisconsin in 1968; Michigan 34, Wisconsin 9.)

49) D – 7 (Neil Snow FB 1902, Robet Chappuis HB 1948, Donald Dufek FB 1951, Mel Anthony FB 1965, Butch Woolfork RB 1981, Leroy Hoard FB 1989, Tyrone Wheatley RB 1993)

50) C – 1897 (Michigan 34, Ohio State 0)

Note: All answers valid as of the end of the 2007 season, unless otherwise indicated in the question itself.

Second Quarter *2-Point Questions*

1) Where did Rich Rodriguez coach before Michigan?

    A) Cincinnati
    B) LSU
    C) Eastern Michigan
    D) West Virginia

2) What is the first score written on the Little Brown Jug?

    A) 0-0
    B) 0-3
    C) 6-6
    D) 24-7

3) How many Michigan defensive players are in the College Football Hall of Fame?

    A) 0
    B) 1
    C) 3
    D) 6

4) How many different decades have the Wolverines won at least 85 games?

    A) 0
    B) 1
    C) 3
    D) 5

Second Quarter *2-Point Questions*

5) Which Michigan head coach has the second most all-time wins?

    A) Bump Elliot
    B) Harry Kipke
    C) Lloyd Carr
    D) Fielding Yost

6) How many undefeated/untied seasons has Michigan had (minimum 8 games)?

    A) 6
    B) 9
    C) 11
    D) 14

7) Who has the most career interceptions for Michigan?

    A) Charles Woodson
    B) Tom Curtis
    C) Tripp Welborne
    D) Ty Law

8) Which U.S. Service Academy has Michigan never played?

    A) Air Force
    B) Navy
    C) Army
    D) Has played all three

9) Which coach had the second longest coaching tenure at Michigan?

    A) Lloyd Carr
    B) Herbert Crisler
    C) Bennie Oosterbaan
    D) Bo Schembechler

10) Which team has Michigan played LESS THAN 75 times?

    A) Michigan State
    B) Illinois
    C) Wisconsin
    D) Minnesota

11) How many Michigan head coaches have won the team MVP Award as Michigan football players?

    A) 0
    B) 2
    C) 4
    D) 6

12) How many Michigan quarterbacks have been named consensus All-American?

    A) 0
    B) 1
    C) 3
    D) 4

13) Who recorded the most sacks for Michigan in 2007?

    A) Jamar Adams
    B) Shawn Crable
    C) Brandon Graham
    D) Tim Jamison

14) How many Michigan players have received the team MVP Award more than once?

    A) 1
    B) 3
    C) 5
    D) 7

15) Who has the Michigan record for most points scored against Ohio State?

    A) Tim Biakabutuka
    B) Tom Harmon
    C) Chris Perry
    D) Anthony Thomas

16) What are the most sacks recorded in a single season by a Michigan player?

    A) 9
    B) 11
    C) 14
    D) 16

17) Which Michigan player has the career record for combined punt returns and kickoff returns for touchdowns in Michigan history?

    A) Desmond Howard
    B) Derrick Alexander
    C) Gil Chapman
    D) Steve Breaston

18) What is the longest winning streak in the Michigan-Ohio State series?

    A) 5
    B) 7
    C) 9
    D) 11

19) How many times has College Gameday visited Ann Arbor?

    A) 6
    B) 9
    C) 11
    D) 15

20) Does Michigan have a winning record in Bowl games?

    A) Yes
    B) No

Second Quarter *2-Point Questions*

WOLVERINEOLOGY TRIVIA CHALLENGE

21) When did the "Go Blue, M Club Supports You" banner first appear on the football field at Michigan Stadium?

    A) 1951
    B) 1957
    C) 1962
    D) 1968

22) What year did Michigan first join the Big Ten (then known as the Western Conference)?

    A) 1896
    B) 1904
    C) 1912
    D) 1920

23) What year did Michigan first travel out of state for a game?

    A) 1879
    B) 1883
    C) 1887
    D) 1890

24) Which non-conference team has UM played the most?

    A) Notre Dame
    B) Case
    C) Chicago
    D) Pennsylvania

25) How many Michigan players have won Rose Bowl MVP (includes all positions)?

   A) 7
   B) 9
   C) 12
   D) 15

26) Who holds the Michigan career record for points scored?

   A) Anthony Thomas
   B) Anthony Carter
   C) Tom Harmon
   D) Desmond Howard

27) Which team gave Michigan its biggest loss?

   A) Ohio State
   B) Cornell
   C) Notre Dame
   D) Yale

28) How many Michigan players have been awarded a Bowl MVP twice?

   A) 0
   B) 2
   C) 4
   D) 8

29) Who was the first 3-time consensus All-American for Michigan?

    A) Tripp Welborne
    B) Anthony Carter
    C) Bennie Oosterbaan
    D) Tom Harmon

30) What year did Michigan not field a team after starting football play in 1879?

    A) 1882
    B) 1886
    C) 1890
    D) 1894

31) Did Tim Biakabutuka have three times as many rushing yards as Heisman Trophy winner Eddie George in the 1995 Michigan-Ohio State game?

    A) Yes
    B) No

32) How many years did Michigan play without a head coach?

    A) 0
    B) 3
    C) 7
    D) 11

33) Did Michigan have a winning record the first season?

    A) Yes
    B) No

34) Which team gave Michigan its first loss?

    A) Harvard
    B) Yale
    C) Toronto
    D) Chicago

35) What was Michigan's first bowl game outside of the Rose Bowl?

    A) Sugar Bowl
    B) Cotton Bowl
    C) Blue Bonnet Bowl
    D) Orange Bowl

36) Who was Michigan's first opponent in Michigan Stadium?

    A) Ohio Wesleyan
    B) Miami, Ohio
    C) Ball State
    D) Florida

Second Quarter
2-Point Questions

37) Who was named as Michigan's first head coach?

   A) Gustave Ferbert
   B) Mike Murphy
   C) Frank Crawford
   D) Fielding Yost

38) How many 3-time consensus All-Americans have played for Michigan?

   A) 1
   B) 3
   C) 5
   D) 7

39) Who is the only Wolverine quarterback to pass for over 3,000 yards in a season?

   A) Tom Brady
   B) Todd Collins
   C) Elvis Grbac
   D) John Navarre

40) Who was the last Michigan player to have been named consensus All-American two times?

   A) Charles Woodson
   B) Michael Hart
   C) Jake Long
   D) Braylon Edwards

41) Who holds the Michigan record for receiving yards in a single game?

    A) Derrick Alexander
    B) Desmond Howard
    C) Jack Clancy
    D) Jim Smith

42) Who was the first consensus All-American defensive back at Michigan?

    A) Charles Woodson
    B) Tom Curtis
    C) Ernest Shazor
    D) Tripp Welborne

43) Who had the longest punt return for Michigan against Ohio State?

    A) Desmond Howard
    B) Anthony Carter
    C) Steve Breaston
    D) Tyrone Wheatley

44) What year did Michigan win its first Big Ten title?

    A) 1898
    B) 1913
    C) 1918
    D) 1925

45) Which team did Gary Moeller say was more of a rival to Michigan than Ohio State?

    A) Michigan State
    B) Notre Dame
    C) Illinois
    D) Penn State

46) Which conference opponent does Michigan have the most wins against?

    A) Northwestern
    B) Indiana
    C) Penn State
    D) Minnesota

47) Which Big 10 team has the most wins against Michigan?

    A) Ohio State
    B) Michigan State
    C) Illinois
    D) Minnesota

48) How many Wolverine quarterbacks have thrown at least 25 touchdown passes in a single season?

    A) 1
    B) 2
    C) 4
    D) 5

49) How many Wolverine head coaches have won National Coach of the Year while at Michigan?

    A) 0
    B) 2
    C) 4
    D) 7

50) How many outright Big Ten Championships has Michigan won?

    A) 7
    B) 10
    C) 15
    D) 18

Second Quarter
Wolverine Cool Fact

Michigan dropped out of the Big Ten in 1907 because of new league rules limiting games to 5 per season and allowing only 3 years varsity status to players. In the 10 years as an independent, Michigan compiled a record of 52-16-7 (.740). The only Big Ten School Michigan played during that period was Minnesota with Michigan winning both meetings, 15-6 in 1909 and 6-0 in 1910.

Second Quarter Answer Key

1) D – West Virginia (Rodriguez coached the Mountaineers from 2001-07 and posted a 60-26 record [.698].)

2) C – 6-6 (Minnesota tied the game with two minutes left and the game was stopped because of the ensuing celebration by the Golden Gophers and their fans.)

3) B – 1 (Tom Curtis, Safety 1967-69, inducted in 2005)

4) C – 3 (96 wins in the 70s; 90 wins in the 80s; 93 wins in the 90s)

5) D – Fielding Yost (165-29-10 [.833])

6) B – 9 (1898, 1901, 1902, 1904, 1923, 1932, 1947, 1948, 1997)

7) B – Tom Curtis (22 interceptions from 1967-69)

8) D – Has played all three (4-5 versus Army, 12-5-1 versus Navy, and 1-0 versus Air Force; 17-10-1 for a combined winning percentage of .625.)

9) D – Bo Schembechler (21 years, 1969-89)

10) C – Wisconsin (Michigan has played the Badgers 61 times and leads the series 48-12-1 [.795].)

11) B – 2 (Bennie Oosterbaan 1927, Bump Elliot 1947)

12) A – 0 (Stunning considering how many NFL quarterbacks the Wolverines have produced.)

13) C – Brandon Graham (Brandon recorded 8.5 sacks in 2007 for a loss of 54 yards.)

14) C – 5 (Michael Hart in 2006-07, Anthony Carter 1980 and 82, Ron Johnson 1967-68, Tom Harmon 1939-40, Ralph Heikkinen 1937-38)

15) B – Tom Harmon (22 points in 1940; Michigan 40, Ohio State 0)

16) B – 12 (LaMarr Woodley recorded 12 sacks for a loss of 119 yards in 2006.)

17) D – Steve Breaston (4 punt returns, 1 kickoff return)

18) C – 9 (Michigan from 1901-1908)

19) B – 9 (Michigan is currently tied in second place with most visits along with Florida. Ohio State is first with 10.)

20) B – No (The Wolverines have a 19-20 record [.487].)

21) C – 1962 (Bump Elliot allowed the banner on the field for homecoming against Illinois.)

22) A – 1896 (Michigan left the conference in 1907 due to conflicts with the Big Ten's decision to limit games played to a total of six per season.)

23) A – 1879 (Michigan actually travel to Chicago for that first matchup against Racine.)

24) A – Notre Dame (35 games)

25) B – 9 (Neil Snow FB 1902, Robet Chappuis HB 1948, Donald Dufek FB 1951, Mel Anthony FB 1965, Rick Leach QB 1979, Buthch Woolfork RB 1981, Leroy Hoard FB 1989, Tyrone Wheatley RB 1993, and Brian Griese QB 1998)

26) A – Anthony Thomas (Thomas recorded 56 touchdowns from 1997-00 [55 rushing, 1 receiving].)

27) B – Cornell (In 1889 Michigan suffered their biggest loss ever to Cornell by 56 points [56-0].)

28) C – 4 (Butch Woolfork 1981 Rose Bowl, 1981 Blue Bonnet Bowl; Jamie Morris 1986 Fiesta Bowl, 1988 Hall of Fame Bowl; Tyrone Wheatley 1993 Rose Bowl, 1994 Hall of Fame Bowl; Anthony Thomas 1999 Citrus Bowl, 2001 Citrus Bowl)

29) C – Bennie Oosterbaan (1925-1927)

30) A – 1882

31) A – Yes (Biakabutuka had 313 yards rushing and George had 104 yards rushing.)

32) D – 11 (The Wolverines played without a coach from 1879-1890. Does not include 1882 when no team was fielded.)

33) A – Yes (The Wolverines beat Racine and tied Toronto to finish the season 1-0-1.)

34) A – Harvard (Harvard beat the Wolverines 1-0 back when a touchdown counted as 1 point.)

35) D – Orange Bowl (The Wolverines fell 6-14 to Oklahoma in the 1976 Orange Bowl.)

36) A – Ohio Wesleyan (The Wolverines won their first game played in Michigan Stadium 33-0 against Ohio Wesleyan.)

37) B – Mike Murphy (Murphy was named the first Wolverine head coach in 1891 and was joined by Frank Crawford mid season.)

38) A – 1 (Bennie Oosterbaan, 1925-27)

39) D – John Navarre (Navarre passed for 3,331 yards in 2003; 270-456 with 24 touchdowns and 10 interceptions.)

40) C – Jake Long (As a Wolverine offensive tackle, Long was a consensus All-American in 2006 and 2007. Michigan has had a total of 12 players named consensus All-American two or more years.)

41) C – Jack Clancy (1966 versus Oregon State, 197 yards on 10 receptions)

42) B – Tom Curtis (In 1969 Curtis had 49 tackles and 6 interceptions.)

43) A – Desmond Howard (Desmond struck his infamous Heisman pose after returning a punt 93 yards for a touchdown against the Buckeyes in 1991. This is also a school punt return record.)

44) A – 1898 (Michigan finished 3-0 in conference play.)

45) A – Michigan State (Moeller felt that the in-state rivalry meant more to Michigan than the Ohio State game.)

46) D – Minnesota (Michigan has 69 wins against Minnesota and leads the series 69-24-3 [.734])

47) A – Ohio State (The Buckeyes have 41 wins against Michigan and the Wolverines lead the series 57-41-6 [.577].)

48) B – 2 (Chad Henne threw 25 touchdown passes in 2004, and Elvis Grbac threw 25 in 1991.)

49) C – 4 (Fritz Crisler 1947, Bennie Oosterbaan 1948, Bo Schembechler 1969, and Lloyd Carr 1997. *Note: All were awarded the American Football Coaches Association [AFCA] Coach of the Year Award.)

50) D – 18 (1898, 1902, 1925, 1932, 1933, 1947, 1948, 1950, 1964, 1971, 1980, 1982, 1988, 1989, 1991, 1992, 1997, & 2003)

Note: All answers valid as of the end of the 2007 season, unless otherwise indicated in the question itself.

1) What section of the Michigan band performs a Stepshow on the steps of Revelli Hall before home games?

- A) Drum line
- B) Trumpet
- C) Saxophone
- D) Flute

2) What year was the first winning season at Michigan (minimum 5 games)?

- A) 1882
- B) 1888
- C) 1899
- D) 1912

3) Against which Big Ten team does Michigan currently have the longest winning streak?

- A) Indiana
- B) Iowa
- C) Northwestern
- D) Penn State

4) What year was the first conference game between Michigan and Ohio State?

- A) 1906
- B) 1912
- C) 1918
- D) 1924

5) What are the most points scored in a game by Michigan?

- A) 90
- B) 110
- C) 130
- D) 150

6) Which Michigan quarterback completed the most passes in a bowl game?

- A) Chris Zurbrugg
- B) Brian Griese
- C) Bob Ptacek
- D) Tom Brady

7) Which non-conference opponent has the most wins against Michigan?

- A) Southern Cal
- B) Notre Dame
- C) Washington
- D) Pennsylvania

8) What is the longest kickoff return for Michigan against Ohio State?

- A) 45 yards
- B) 60 yards
- C) 75 yards
- D) 90 yards

9) Which Wolverine kicker holds the top three spots for longest field goal in a game?

    A) Garrett Rivas
    B) Hayden Epstein
    C) Kraig Baker
    D) Adam Finley

10) Michigan running backs have rushed for over 1,000 yards in a season over 25 times.

    A) True
    B) False

11) Who holds the Michigan record for the most punts of 50 yards or more in a career?

    A) Zoltan Mesko
    B) Ross Ryan
    C) Adam Finley
    D) Jason Vinson

12) Who holds the Michigan record for receiving yards in a career?

    A) Mercury Hayes
    B) Braylon Edwards
    C) Tai Streets
    D) Anthony Carter

13) What is the Michigan record for tackles for loss in one season?

   A) 19.5
   B) 23
   C) 28.5
   D) 33

14) When was the first year Michigan played a home game?

   A) 1879
   B) 1881
   C) 1883
   D) 1887

15) What is the largest margin of victory for Michigan against Ohio State?

   A) 35
   B) 42
   C) 69
   D) 86

16) How many points were scored against Fielding Yost's Michigan teams in the 204 games he coached?

   A) 674
   B) 800
   C) 950
   D) 1,324

17) What year did the infamous Snow Bowl take place between Michigan and Ohio State?

    A) 1945
    B) 1950
    C) 1955
    D) 1960

18) The Wolverines have never scored more than 500 points in a season.

    A) True
    B) False

19) How many seasons has Michigan gone undefeated at home?

    A) 35
    B) 41
    C) 49
    D) 54

20) What are the most consecutive wins for Michigan in the Little Brown Jug game?

    A) 5
    B) 8
    C) 13
    D) 16

21) Which coach has the best winning percentage at Michigan (min. 3 seasons)?

    A) William Ward
    B) Bo Schembechler
    C) Fielding Yost
    D) Gary Moeller

22) Has Michigan played every Pac 10 team at least once?

    A) Yes
    B) No

23) How many Michigan players are in the College Football Hall of Fame for more than one position?

    A) 0
    B) 2
    C) 4
    D) 6

24) Who was the first consensus All-American wide receiver at Michigan?

    A) Braylon Edwards
    B) Anthony Carter
    C) Desmond Howard
    D) Derrick Alexander

25) What are planted next to each foot on the Paul Bunyan trophy?

    A) United States flag & Michigan State flag
    B) Pine trees
    C) Oak trees
    D) UM flag & Michigan State University flag

26) Who was UM's first consensus All-American linebacker?

    A) Mike Taylor
    B) Ron Simpkins
    C) Jarrett Irons
    D) Tom Stincic

27) Who holds the UM season record for receiving yards?

    A) Anthony Carter
    B) David Terrell
    C) Amani Toomer
    D) Braylon Edwards

28) Who was the only player to receive consensus All-American honors in the 1950s?

    A) Ron Kramer
    B) Bill Yearby
    C) Dan Dierdorf
    D) Jim Mandich

29) Has a Michigan ever quarterback passed for over 10,000 yards in a career?

    A) Yes
    B) No

30) What was the winning percentage of coaches that lasted one season at Michigan?

    A) .497
    B) .566
    C) .633
    D) .716

31) Who holds the Michigan record for points scored in a season?

    A) Desmond Howard
    B) Anthony Thomas
    C) Anthony Carter
    D) Chris Perry

32) How many times have Michigan players finished second in the Heisman voting?

    A) 2
    B) 3
    C) 5
    D) 6

33) How many times has Michigan finished last in the Big Ten?

    A) 0
    B) 3
    C) 5
    D) 7

34) How many years did Tom Harmon lead the nation in all purpose yards?

    A) 0
    B) 1
    C) 2
    D) 3

35) What are Michigan's most consecutive Big Ten titles?

    A) 3
    B) 5
    C) 6
    D) 9

36) What are UM's most consecutive bowl losses?

    A) 2
    B) 5
    C) 7
    D) 9

WOLVERINEOLOGY TRIVIA CHALLENGE

37) How many losses did Michigan have going into the historic 1969 game versus #1 ranked Ohio State?

    A) 1
    B) 2
    C) 4
    D) 5

38) What was the name of Michigan's first home?

    A) Regents Field
    B) Ann Arbor Fairgrounds
    C) Tiger Stadium
    D) Wayne County Fairgrounds

39) How many times has Michigan shut out their opponent?

    A) 235
    B) 287
    C) 327
    D) 341

40) What is Michigan's longest drought between bowl appearances since 1948?

    A) 1 years
    B) 5 years
    C) 9 years
    D) 13 years

MICHIGAN WOLVERINES FOOTBALL

41) What are the most consecutive bowl games Michigan has won?

    A) 2
    B) 4
    C) 6
    D) 9

42) Who is the oldest college football player to be named consensus All-American?

    A) Alvin Wistert
    B) Bill Yearby
    C) Marlin Jackson
    D) Jim Elliot

43) How many combined rushing and passing yards did Michigan have in the Snow Bowl?

    A) 27
    B) 41
    C) 52
    D) 60

44) Who coached Michigan in their first Big Ten Season?

    A) Langdon Lea
    B) Fielding Yost
    C) William Ward
    D) Bump Elliot

45) Who was the first conference opponent for Michigan?

    A) Ohio State
    B) Penn State
    C) Indiana
    D) Purdue

46) How many Michigan players have been named first team Academic All-American?

    A) 17
    B) 20
    C) 23
    D) 28

47) Where did Michigan play before Michigan Stadium?

    A) Ferry Field
    B) Regents Field
    C) Maize Stadium
    D) Ann Arbor Fairgrounds

48) What is Michigan's longest drought between Big Ten Championships?

    A) 7 years
    B) 9 years
    C) 11 years
    D) 13 years

Third Quarter *3-Point Questions*

49) Who was Michigan's 800th overall win against?

    A) Ohio State
    B) Northwestern
    C) Central Michigan
    D) Wisconsin

50) What was the most rushing yards gained by the Wolverines in a single game in 2007?

    A) 270
    B) 294
    C) 307
    D) 323

Third Quarter Wolverine Cool Fact

Up until 1901, many of the Wolverines' big games were played on the field of the Detroit Athletic Club to accommodate all of the alumni who wanted to see their team in action. Michigan's 1895 game against Minnesota was held at the Detroit Baseball Park, which Michigan won 20 to 0. The last game played there was in 1901. That game ended in a Wolverine win against Carlisle (Michigan 22, Carlisle 0).

Third Quarter Answer Key

1) A – Drum Line (The drum line performs on the steps of Revelli Hall about 1:30 before each home game.)

2) B – 1888 (4-1)

3) A – Indiana (Michigan has beaten the Hoosiers 15 straight meetings and leads the overall series 50-9 [.847].)

4) C – 1918 (Michigan left the Big Ten in 1907 and did not rejoin until 1917. Ohio State was not a member until 1913.)

5) C – 130 (In 1904 Michigan beat West Virginia 130-0.)

6) D – Tom Brady (Brady completed 34 passes against Alabama in the 2000 Orange Bowl; Michigan 35, Alabama 34.)

7) B – Notre Dame (The Irish have 14 wins against UM; Michigan leads the series 20-14-1 [.586].)

8) D – 90 yards (Dave Raimey, 1961)

9) B – Hayden Epstein (Hayden kicked the three longest field goals in Wolverine history; 57 yarder in 2001 vs Michigan State, 56 yarder in 1999 vs Michigan State, 52 yarder in 2000 vs Northwestern.)

10) A – True (17 RBs have rushed over 1,000 yards in a season 28 times; Ranging from Michael Hart in 2004, 2006, and 2007 to Billy Taylor in 1971.)

11) C – Adam Finley (Adam had 31 punts of 50 yards or more from 2001-04; the longest was 68-yards.)

12) B – Braylon Edwards (3,541 yards on 252 receptions, 14.1 yards per reception with 39 touchdowns)

13) C – 28.5 (Shawn Crable, 2007)

14) C – 1883 (The Wolverines did not have a home game until their fourth season of play.)

15) D – 86 (Michigan beat the Buckeyes 86-0 in 1902.)

16) B – 800 (That's only 3.9 points given up per game!)

17) B – 1950 (The Snow Bowl was played in blizzard conditions and the game decided the Big Ten Rose Bowl representative. The Wolverines didn't even gain a first down for the game; Michigan 9, Ohio State 3.)

18) B – False (Michigan scored a total of 644 points in 1902 [58.5 per game average]. The closest the Wolverines have gotten since then is 460 points in 2003.)

19) D – 54 (The last time was in 2006.)

20) D – 16 (Michigan won every meeting from 1987 through 2004.)

21) B – Bo Schembechler (143-24-3, .850)

22) A – Yes (Michigan has an overall record of 44-21-1 against the Pac 10 [.674].)

23) B – 2 (Merv Pregulman for tackle and center; Neil Snow for end and fullback.)

24) B – Anthony Carter (Anthony was first named consensus All-American in 1981 and had 50 receptions for 952 yards and 8 touchdowns. He was also named consensus All-American in 1982 with 43 receptions for 844 yards and 8 TDs.)

25) D – University of Michigan flag & Michigan State University flag

26) A – Mike Taylor (In 1971 Taylor had 97 tackles, 7 pass breakups, and 2 interceptions.)

27) D – Braylon Edwards (1,330 yards on 97 receptions, 13.7 yards per reception with 15 touchdowns)

28) A – Ron Kramer (Kramer was twice named consensus All-American in the 1950s. In 1955 Kramer had 12 receptions for 224 yards and 4 touchdowns, 1956 Kramer had 18 receptions for 353 yards and 2 touchdowns as an end.)

29) B – No (John Navarre came the closest with 9,254 yards over his career.)

30) D – .716 (One year head coaches finished 26-10-1.)

31) A – Desmond Howard (Desmond reached the endzone 23 times in 1991; 2 rushing, 19 receiving, 1 kickoff return, 1 punt return.)

32) A – 2 (Tom Harmon in 1939 [winner was Nile Kinnick from Iowa] and Bob Chappuis in 1947 [winner was John Lujack from Notre Dame].)

33) B – 3 (1934 0-6, 1-7; 1936 0-5 1-7; 1962 1-6 2-7)

34) C – 2 (1939 1,208 yards; 1940 1,312 yards)

35) B – 5 (1988-1992)

36) C – 7 (1970 and 1972 Rose Bowls, 1976 Orange Bowl, 1977-79 Rose Bowls, and 1979 Gator Bowl)

37) B – 2 (The Wolverines had previous losses to #7 Missouri and unranked Michigan State.)

38) B – Ann Arbor Fairgrounds

39) D – 341 (That is 28.9% of the total games played by the Wolverines. Last time was in 2007 against Notre Dame; Michigan 38, ND 0.)

40) D – 13 years (The Wolverines did not participate in a bowl game from 1952-1964.)

41) B – 4 (two different times; 1902, 1948, 1951, 1965 Rose Bowls and again 1998 Rose Bowl, 1999 Citrus Bowl, 2000 Orange Bowl, 2001 Citrus Bowl)

42) A – Alvin Wistert (Alvin played tackle for the Wolverines and was named consensus All-American in 1948-49. Alvin was 33 years old in 1949.)

43) A – 27 (The Wolverines had 0 yards passing on 9 attempts and 27 yards rushing. The top rusher for Michigan was Ralph Stratton with 14 yards on twelve carries.)

44) C – William Ward (Michigan finished 2-1 the first Big Ten season.)

45) D – Purdue (1896 at Purdue, Michigan 16   Purdue 0)

46) A – 17 (The last player to be named first team
   Academic All-American was nose tackle Rob
   Renes in 1999.)

47) A – Ferry Field (The Wolverines played on Ferry Field
   from 1902-1926.)

48) D – 13 years (Michigan did not win a Big Ten
   Championship from 1951-1963.)

49) D – Wisconsin (Michigan recorded its 800th victory at
   home against the Badgers on September 30th,
   2000 [Michigan 13, Wisconsin 10].)

50) C – 307 (Brandon Minor and Carlos Brown each had
   100 yard games as the Wolverines pounded out 3
   rushing touchdowns and beat the Golden
   Gophers 22-16.)

Note: All answers valid as of the end of the 2007
season, unless otherwise indicated in the question
itself.

WOLVERINEOLOGY TRIVIA CHALLENGE

1) What is the longest win streak for either Michigan or Michigan State in the Paul Bunyan Game?

A) 4
B) 6
C) 8
D) 10

2) How many former Michigan players have been inducted into the Pro Football Hall of Fame?

A) 5
B) 7
C) 9
D) 11

3) How many teams does Michigan have at least 50 wins against?

A) 1
B) 3
C) 5
D) 7

4) The Wolverines have had two 100 yard rushers in more than 25 games.

A) True
B) False

MICHIGAN WOLVERINES FOOTBALL

Fourth Quarter *4-Point Questions*

5) How many jersey numbers has Michigan retired?

    A) 5
    B) 6
    C) 8
    D) 9

6) What is the largest margin of victory for Michigan over Notre Dame?

    A) 14 points
    B) 38 points
    C) 52 points
    D) 65 points

7) Excluding Michigan State, who is the last school from Michigan to beat the Wolverines?

    A) Albion
    B) Eastern Michigan
    C) Kalamazoo
    D) No team

8) How many ex-Michigan head coaches are in the College Football Hall of Fame?

    A) 1
    B) 3
    C) 5
    D) 7

Fourth Quarter *4-Point Questions*

9) What number did Bo Schembechler make the scout team wear before the Ohio State game in 1969?

    A) No number
    B) 1
    C) 50
    D) 99

10) When was the last time Michigan was shutout?

    A) 1984
    B) 1990
    C) 1996
    D) 2002

11) Under which coach was the Michigan record set for consecutive conference wins?

    A) Gary Moeller
    B) Fritz Crisler
    C) Bo Schembechler
    D) Fielding Yost

12) How many shutouts did Michigan have under Coach Fielding Yost?

    A) 73
    B) 93
    C) 113
    D) 133

Fourth Quarter *4-Point Questions*

13) What decade did Michigan have the best winning percentage?

    A) 1900s
    B) 1910s
    C) 1940s
    D) 1970s

14) Who holds the Michigan single season rushing record?

    A) Tim Biakabutuka
    B) Anthony Thomas
    C) Tony Boles
    D) Ricky Powers

15) Which team has Michigan played the most to open the season?

    A) Michigan State
    B) Case
    C) Eastern Michigan
    D) Miami, OH

16) Who was the first opponent to draw over 100,000 fans into Michigan Stadium?

    A) Ohio State
    B) Michigan State
    C) Indiana
    D) Notre Dame

Fourth Quarter *4-Point Questions*

17) What were the names of the two live wolverines that were on display for Michigan Stadium's dedication in 1927?

    A) Bennie and Biff
    B) Spartan and Buckeye eaters
    C) Tom and Jerry
    D) Abbott and Costello

18) How many points did Michigan score in the fourth quarter against Minnesota in 2003?

    A) 21
    B) 28
    C) 31
    D) 35

19) Who led the nation in field goals made in 1994?

    A) Remy Hamilton
    B) Kraig Baker
    C) Peter Elezovic
    D) John Carlson

20) Who has the most receptions for Michigan in a single game against Ohio State?

    A) Brad Myers
    B) Braylon Edwards
    C) Marquise Walker
    D) Tai Streets

Fourth Quarter *4-Point Questions*

21) How many head coaches has Michigan had?

    A) 12
    B) 14
    C) 17
    D) 20

22) What are the most consecutive losses for Michigan in the Little Brown Jug game?

    A) 3
    B) 7
    C) 9
    D) 12

23) Which coach has the second best winning percentage at Michigan (min. 3 seasons)?

    A) Fielding Yost
    B) Lloyd Carr
    C) Bump Elliot
    D) Bennie Oosterbaan

24) Does Michigan have more than a .750 all time winning percentage in Big Ten play?

    A) Yes
    B) No

Fourth Quarter *4-Point Questions*

25) Why has Michigan Stadium's capacity always ended in the number 1 since 1956?

    A)   Indicates first place in stadium size
    B)   One seat is always left for ex-Coach Fritz Crisler
    C)   The top row always has to end in an odd number
    D)   Signifies the quest to be the best

26) What is Michigan's all-time win total?

    A)   848
    B)   856
    C)   869
    D)   874

27) Who holds the Rose Bowl record for touchdowns and points scored in a single game?

    A)   Neil Snow
    B)   Tyrone Wheatley
    C)   Chris Perry
    D)   Bob Westfall

28) How many Michigan players have won the Outland Trophy?

    A)   0
    B)   1
    C)   3
    D)   5

WOLVERINEOLOGY TRIVIA CHALLENGE

29) What decade did Michigan have the worst winning percentage?

    A) 1930s
    B) 1950s
    C) 1960s
    D) 1990s

30) What was the largest margin of victory for Michigan in a bowl game?

    A) 19 points
    B) 29 points
    C) 39 points
    D) 49 points

31) How many Michigan players are in the College Football Hall of Fame?

    A) 22
    B) 28
    C) 32
    D) 36

32) What position did Rich Rodriguez play in college?

    A) Linebacker
    B) Tackle
    C) Tight End
    D) Defensive Back

MICHIGAN WOLVERINES FOOTBALL

Fourth Quarter *4-Point Questions*

33) How many decades has Michigan won at least 80% of their games?

    A) 0
    B) 1
    C) 3
    D) 5

34) What team gave Michigan its worst defeat suffered in a bowl game?

    A) Southern Cal
    B) Tennessee
    C) Washington
    D) BYU

35) Who holds the Rose Bowl rushing record for Michigan?

    A) Tyrone Wheatley
    B) Leroy Hoard
    C) Chris Perry
    D) Anthony Thomas

36) How many times has Michigan appeared in the Orange/Sugar/Fiesta/Rose bowls combined?

    A) 14
    B) 19
    C) 25
    D) 29

Fourth Quarter *4-Point Questions*

37) What was the best winning percentage of a Michigan head coach that lasted only one season?

    A) .525
    B) .650
    C) .775
    D) .900

38) How many years did Michigan play a double-header to open the season?

    A) Never
    B) 1
    C) 3
    D) 5

39) How many Michigan Linebackers have won bowl MVP?

    A) 0
    B) 1
    C) 3
    D) 5

40) How many Michigan players have won the Lombardi Award?

    A) 1
    B) 2
    C) 4
    D) 5

41) What is the Michigan record for consecutive games without a loss?

- A) 11
- B) 26
- C) 41
- D) 56

42) How many times did Elvis Grbac lead the nation in passing efficiency?

- A) 0
- B) 1
- C) 2
- D) 3

43) Which Michigan player received the most individual national awards in a single year?

- A) Charles Woodson
- B) Tom Harmon
- C) Desmond Howard
- D) Erick Anderson

44) Which rushing category did Michael Hart lead the Big Ten in 2007?

- A) Total attempts
- B) Average yards per game
- C) Total yards
- D) Touchdowns

WOLVERINEOLOGY TRIVIA CHALLENGE

45) How many first round NFL Draft picks has Michigan produced?

   A) 35
   B) 39
   C) 42
   D) 50

46) Did Lloyd Carr ever win Big Ten Coach of the Year?

   A) Yes
   B) No

47) How many Michigan players have been selected as Big Ten Freshman of the Year?

   A) 1
   B) 3
   C) 4
   D) 6

48) What is the Michigan record for most consecutive wins without ties?

   A) 29
   B) 35
   C) 41
   D) 59

49) What is the only defensive category the 1997 Michigan Wolverines did not lead the nation in?

    A) Scoring defense
    B) Total defense
    C) Passing defense
    D) Rushing defense

50) How many Michigan coaches and players are in the Rose Bowl Hall of Fame?

    A) 2
    B) 4
    C) 6
    D) 9

Fourth Quarter Wolverine Cool Fact

In 1940 Tom Harmon book ended the season with spectacular performances. In the season opener against California he ran back the opening kickoff for a touchdown, returned a punt for a touchdown, had two rushing touchdowns, and a passing touchdown. As if this were not enough, he kicked four extra points. In the final game of the season at Ohio State Harmon threw two passing touchdowns, ran for three touchdowns, and kicked four extra points. He also punted three times for an average of 50 yards per punt, and had three interceptions on defense. Give this man a Heisman!

Fourth Quarter Answer Key

1) C – 8 (Michigan won every meeting from 1970-77.)

2) B – 7 (Benny Friedman inducted in 2005, George Allen in 2002, Tom Mack in 1999, Dan Dierdorf in 1996, Len Ford in 1976, Bill Hewitt in 1971, and Elroy Hirsh in 1968.)

3) C – 5 (Ohio State 57, Michigan State 67, Minnesota 69, Illinois 66, and Northwestern 51)

4) A – True (Michigan has had two 100 yard rushers in a game 34 times with the last time against Minnesota in 2007. The Wolverines are 33-1 in those games.)

5) A – 5 (#ll for the Wistert brothers, Tom Harmon's #98, Ron Kramer's #87, Gerald Ford's #48, and Bennie Oosterbaan's #47.)

6) B – 38 points (The Wolverines have beaten the Irish two times [2003, 2007] by 38 points; Michigan 38, Notre Dame 0.)

7) D – No team (No team from Michigan other than the Spartans has beaten the Wolverines.)

8) C – 5 (Fielding Yost, George Little, Tad Wieman, Fritz Crisler, and Bo Schembechler)

9) C – 50 (Schembechler made the scout team wear this number to constantly remind the players of the 50 points scored against them by Ohio State in 1968.)

74

10) A – 1984 (The Wolverines were shutout in Iowa 0-26. That makes 288 games since Michigan was last shutout! The Wolverines have only been shutout a total of 75 times in school history.)

11) A – Gary Moeller (19 consecutive Big Ten wins from 1990-1992)

12) C – 113 (55.4% of his 204 games coached.)

13) A – 1900s (82-8-3, .898)

14) A – Tim Biakabutuka (1,818 yards in 1995 on 303 carries with 12 touchdowns)

15) B – Case (Played in 16 season openings, last meeting in 1923; Michigan's record in those season openers is 15-0-1.)

16) B – Michigan State (In 1956 over 100,000 fans filled Michigan Stadium for the first time only to watch a 0-9 shutout at the hands of the Spartans.)

17) A – Bennie and Biff (The wolverines were on loan from the Detroit Zoo but it was decided these animals proved too ferocious to keep. However, while Bennie was returned, Biff was kept at the University of Michigan Zoo for students to visit.)

18) C – 31 (Michigan scored 31 points in the fourth quarter to win 38-35 at Minnesota.)

19) A – Remy Hamilton (24-29, .828)

20) C – Marquise Walker (15 receptions in 2001 for 160 yards and 2 touchdowns)

21) C – 17

22) C – 9 (Michigan lost the trophy game from 1934 to 1942.)

23) B – Lloyd Carr (75-21, .781)

24) B – No (It's close! The Wolverines are 461-166-18 all time in conference play for a .729 winning percentage.)

25) B – One seat is always left for ex-Coach Fritz Crisler (This tradition started in 1956 with the location of the seat remaining a secret.)

26) C – 869 (The Wolverines all-time record is 869-286-36 for a .745 winning percentage. These are also the most wins of any college football program regardless of division.)

27) A – Neil Snow (Snow scored 5 touchdowns against Stanford in the 1902 Rose Bowl. Back then touchdowns counted as 5 points. His 25 point total still holds as a Rose Bowl scoring record.)

28) A – 0

29) C – 1960s (55-40-2, .577)

30) D – 49 points (On two occasions: 1902 Rose Bowl Michigan 49, Stanford 0; and the 1948 Rose Bowl Michigan 49, Southern Cal 0.)

31) B – 28 (Dave Brown who played safety for the Wolverines from 1972-74 is the most recent inductee [2007].)

32) D – Defensive Back (Rodriguez played for West Virginia from 1981-84. Initially he was a walk on but later earned a scholarship.)

33) C – 3 (1900s, 82-8-3 .898; 1940s 74-15-3 .821; 1970s 96-16-3 .848)

34) B – Tennessee (The Wolverines went down 17-45 to the Volunteers in the 2002 Citrus Bowl.)

35) A – Tyrone Wheatley (235 yards in 1993 on 15 carries and three touchdowns. He was 12 yards from tying the Rose Bowl record of 247 yards set by Charles White of Southern Cal but had to leave the game early due to cramps.)

36) C – 25 (20 Rose Bowls, 2 Orange Bowls, 1 Fiesta Bowl, 1 Sugar Bowl)

37) D – .900 (William Ward, 1896, 9-1)

38) C – 3 (Michigan played double-headers in 1929-31 and went 6-0 in those games, outscoring opponents 156-6.)

39) B – 1 (Sam Sword, 1999 Citrus Bowl; Michigan 45, Arkansas 31)

40) A – 1 (LaMarr Woodley, 2006)

41) D – 56 (From Sept. 28th, 1901 until Nov. 25, 1905; all under Coach Fielding Yost. The Wolverines went 55-0-1 during this stretch.)

42) C – 2 (1991, 169.0 rating, 1,955 yards, 24 touchdowns, 5 interceptions, and 66.7% completion percentage; 1992, 154.2 rating, 1,465 yards, 15 touchdowns, 12 interceptions, and 66.3% completion percentage)

43) A – Charles Woodson (1997, Bednarik, Heisman, Thorpe, Nagurski, and Walter Camp)

44) B – Average yards per game (Hart averaged 136.1 yards per game. Rashard Mendenhall from Illinois was second with a 129.3 yards per game average.)

45) C – 42 (This includes first round pick Jake Long from the 2008 NFL Draft.)

46) B – No (Lloyd Carr was never named Big Ten Coach of the Year. Joe Tiller from Purdue won in 1997, the year the Wolverines won the national title.)

47) C – 4 (Charles Woodson in 1995 by the coaches, Anthony Thomas in 1997 by the coaches and media, Steve Breaston in 2003 by the coaches, and Michael Hart in 2004 by the coaches and media.)

48) A – 29 (Fielding Yost's teams won 29 straight without ties from 1901-1903.)

49) D – Rushing Defense (The 1997 team led the nation in scoring defense, 8.9 points per game; total defense, 206.9 yards per game; and passing defense with a rating of 75.8 & 116 ypg giving up only 4 passing touchdowns with 22 interceptions.)

50) C – 6 (Mel Anthony, Butch Woofolk, Bo Schembechler, Bob Chappuis, Neil Snow, and Bump Elliot)

Note: All answers valid as of the end of the 2007 season, unless otherwise indicated in the question itself.

Overtime Bonus *4-Point Questions*

1) How many times has Michigan led the nation in scoring defense?

    A) 2
    B) 3
    C) 5
    D) 6

2) How many times has Michigan begun the season ranked number one in the first *AP* poll?

    A) 1
    B) 3
    C) 5
    D) 7

3) What year had the most individual national honors awarded to Michigan players?

    A) 1994
    B) 1997
    C) 2003
    D) 2006

4) Who led the nation in passing efficiency in 1985?

    A) Jim Harbaugh
    B) Ken Sollom
    C) Gerald White
    D) Greg McMurty

Overtime Bonus *4-Point Questions*

5) How many Wolverines have been picked number one overall in the NFL Draft?

    A) 1
    B) 2
    C) 4
    D) 5

6) How many years has Michigan led the nation in rushing defense?

    A) 2
    B) 3
    D) 6
    C) 11

7) What are the most consecutive years the Michigan-Ohio State game decided who would go to the Rose Bowl?

    A) 5
    B) 7
    C) 8
    D) 10

8) Which game did Fritz Crisler say was the greatest upset he had ever seen?

    A) UM victory over Cal in the 1951 Rose Bowl
    B) UM victory over #1 ranked Ohio State in 1969
    C) UM loss to unranked Purdue in 1976
    D) UM loss to unranked Wisconsin in 1981

WOLVERINEOLOGY TRIVIA CHALLENGE

9) Which non-conference opponent does Michigan have the most wins against?

    A) Notre Dame
    B) UCLA
    C) Case
    D) Chicago

10) Which Michigan coach was the first in college football to use motion as a decoy?

    A) Harry Kipke
    B) Fritz Crisler
    C) Fielding Yost
    D) Elton Wieman

Overtime Bonus Answer Key

1) D – 6 ('48 4.9 pts/gm, '71 6.4 pts/gm, '72 5.2 pts/gm, '74 6.8 pts/gm, '85 6.8 pts/gm, & '97 8.9 pts/gm)

2) B – 3 (1949, 1981, 1989)

3) B – 1997 (5, all won by Charles Woodson; Bednarik, Heisman, Thorpe, Nagurski, and Walter Camp)

4) A – Jim Harbaugh (163.7 rating, 1,913 yards, 18 TDs, 6 interceptions, and 65.6% completion percentage)

5) B – 2 (Tom Harmon was drafted number one overall by the Bears in 1941 and Jake Long was the top draft pick in 2008 by the Dolphins.)

6) A – 2 (In 1971 the defense gave up 63.3 yards rushing/gm & 3 rushing TDs that season; 2006 the defense gave up 43.4 yards rushing/gm & only 5 rushing TDs.)

7) D – 10 (Michigan-Ohio State decided the Rose Bowl representative every year from 1972-81.)

8) B – Michigan's upset of top ranked Ohio State in 1969

9) C – Case (Though UM leads the series 26-0-1 [.981].)

10) C – Fielding Yost

Note: All answers valid as of the end of the 2007 season, unless otherwise indicated in the question itself.

Player / Team Score Sheet

WOLVERINEOLOGY TRIVIA CHALLENGE

Name:_____

First Quarter		Second Quarter		Third Quarter		Fourth Quarter		Overtime
1	26	1	26	1	26	1	26	1
2	27	2	27	2	27	2	27	2
3	28	3	28	3	28	3	28	3
4	29	4	29	4	29	4	29	4
5	30	5	30	5	30	5	30	5
6	31	6	31	6	31	6	31	6
7	32	7	32	7	32	7	32	7
8	33	8	33	8	33	8	33	8
9	34	9	34	9	34	9	34	9
10	35	10	35	10	35	10	35	10
11	36	11	36	11	36	11	36	
12	37	12	37	12	37	12	37	
13	38	13	38	13	38	13	38	
14	39	14	39	14	39	14	39	
15	40	15	40	15	40	15	40	
16	41	16	41	16	41	16	41	
17	42	17	42	17	42	17	42	
18	43	18	43	18	43	18	43	
19	44	19	44	19	44	19	44	
20	45	20	45	20	45	20	45	
21	46	21	46	21	46	21	46	
22	47	22	47	22	47	22	47	
23	48	23	48	23	48	23	48	
24	49	24	49	24	49	24	49	
25	50	25	50	25	50	25	50	
___x 1 =___		___x 2 =___		___x 3 =___		___x 4 =___		___x 4 =___

Multiply total number correct by point value/quarter to calculate totals for each quarter.

Add total of all quarters below.

Total Points:_____

Thank you for playing Wolverineology Trivia Challenge.

Additional score sheets are available at:
www.TriviaGameBooks.com

85

Player / Team Score Sheet

Name:_____

First Quarter		Second Quarter		Third Quarter		Fourth Quarter		Overtime	
1	26	1	26	1	26	1	26	1	
2	27	2	27	2	27	2	27	2	
3	28	3	28	3	28	3	28	3	
4	29	4	29	4	29	4	29	4	
5	30	5	30	5	30	5	30	5	
6	31	6	31	6	31	6	31	6	
7	32	7	32	7	32	7	32	7	
8	33	8	33	8	33	8	33	8	
9	34	9	34	9	34	9	34	9	
10	35	10	35	10	35	10	35	10	
11	36	11	36	11	36	11	36		
12	37	12	37	12	37	12	37		
13	38	13	38	13	38	13	38		
14	39	14	39	14	39	14	39		
15	40	15	40	15	40	15	40		
16	41	16	41	16	41	16	41		
17	42	17	42	17	42	17	42		
18	43	18	43	18	43	18	43		
19	44	19	44	19	44	19	44		
20	45	20	45	20	45	20	45		
21	46	21	46	21	46	21	46		
22	47	22	47	22	47	22	47		
23	48	23	48	23	48	23	48		
24	49	24	49	24	49	24	49		
25	50	25	50	25	50	25	50		
___ x 1 =___		___ x 2 =___		___ x 3 =___		___ x 4 =___		___ x 4 =___	

Multiply total number correct by point value/quarter to calculate totals for each quarter.

Add total of all quarters below.

Total Points:_____

Thank you for playing Wolverineology Trivia Challenge.

Additional score sheets are available at:
www.TriviaGameBooks.com

87